8-23			
1-15-92			
12-19-92			
2-28-94			

GOOSEBERRIES TO ORANGES

GOOSEBERRIES TO ORANGES

words by *BARBARA COHEN*
pictures by *BEVERLY BRODSKY*

Lothrop, Lee, & Shepard Books · New York

To Frances Rosdol Brodsky—B.C.

To my mother
and the memory of my father
whose stories of the old country
inspired the creation of this book—B.B.

Library of Congress Cataloging in Publication Data
Cohen, Barbara.   Gooseberries to oranges.
Summary: A young girl reminisces about the journey from her cholera-
ravaged village in Russia to the United States where she is reunited with
her father.   [1. United States—Emigration and immigration—
Fiction]   I. Brodsky, Beverly.   II. Title.
PZ7.C6595Go   [E]   81-5774
ISBN 0-688-00690-6   AACR2   ISBN 0-688-00691-4 (lib. bdg.)

Listen, darlings, and I'll tell you a story about what happened to me when I was a little girl.

I lived far away, in Europe, in a village named Rohatyn. My mother was dead. My father had gone to America. I lived with Aunt Rebecca. She couldn't have loved me more if I had been her own child.

My cousin Leah loved me too. She had blue eyes and white skin, like an angel. She washed my hair. She took me for walks. In the spring we picked wild strawberries from the fields. In the summer we ate gooseberries right off the bushes. In the fall we sucked brown pears that grew on trees in front of Aunt Rebecca's little house.

But winter came, and war. We put feather pillows around the walls of the rooms so if bullets hit our house they wouldn't hurt us. Soldiers in steel helmets searched every corner, looking for boys to take away to the army. They tore the mezzuzah off the door jamb because they thought gold was hidden inside. There was no gold inside the mezzuzah, only a little scroll inscribed with words from the Bible.

We had nothing to eat. The well became polluted. An epidemic of cholera roared through Rohatyn. Aunt Rebecca died. Cousin Leah died. Half the village died. I was eight.

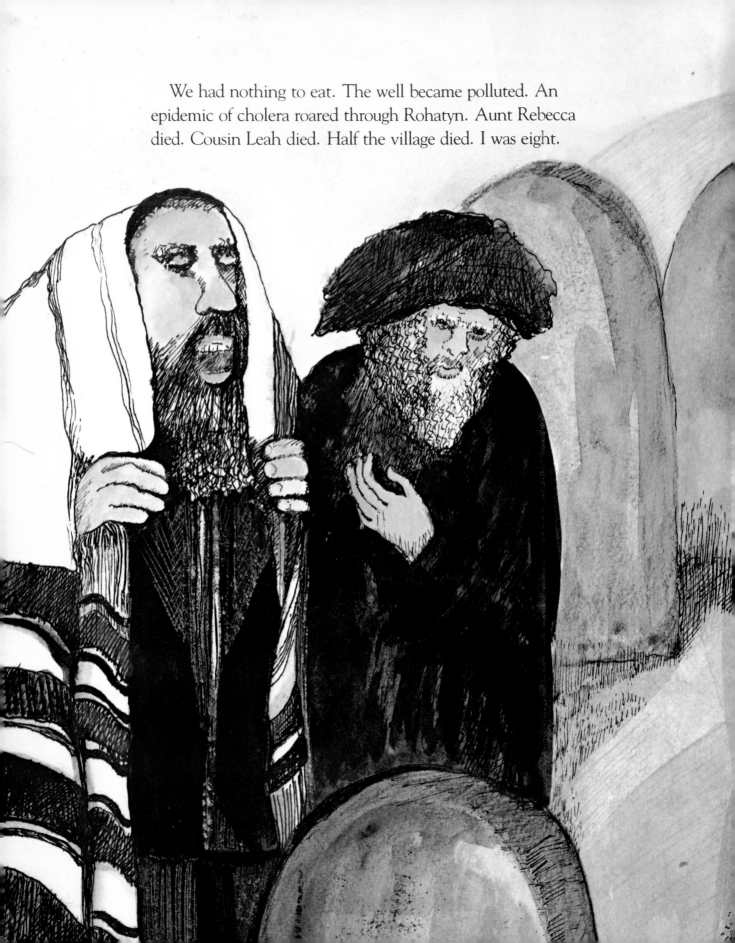

A letter arrived from Papa. "America is the golden land," he said. "Here is a ticket so that you can come to America too."

Did I want to leave my village? Did I want to leave the gooseberries and the little brown pears? But when my Aunt Elke came to get me, I went. So did Aunt Elke's children, Cousin Sylvia, Cousin Sam, Cousin Rose, and Cousin Betty.

The ship carried more people than lived in our whole village. The six of us stayed in a tiny little cubbyhole down deep inside the ship. It had no windows. There were no beds to sleep on, only hammocks, and nothing to eat except moldy bread and Swiss cheese.

Every day on the deck I saw a man studying from a book or rocking back and forth in prayer. He never spoke to me, but I liked to look at him. Papa had written that in America everyone could get an education. Everyone could be learned.

One day I saw another man holding a round, bright thing. "What kind of little ball is that?" I asked him.

"It's not a ball," the man said. "It's an orange. It's to eat." Very slowly, very carefully, he peeled away the skin. Underneath the bumpy skin were plump, juicy sections of fruit. He threw the skin over the railing and into the ocean. He pulled one section away from the others and popped it into his mouth. He chewed it slowly, and then he swallowed it. He did that with another section and another section and another section until the whole orange was gone.

A few days later I saw the orange man again. "Have you seen the man with the book?" I asked him.

"Didn't you hear?" the orange man said. "He threw himself overboard. He drowned."

"Why?" I cried. "Why did he do that?"

The orange man shrugged. "He was very sick. He was coughing blood. He knew that when he got to America they would send him back. He decided he'd rather be dead."

Every night I prayed that I wouldn't get sick, and that Aunt Elke and Sylvia, Sam, Rose, and Betty wouldn't get sick.

The ship pulled into New York harbor. We passed the Statue of Liberty. All the passengers stood on the deck and cheered.

We came to Ellis Island. Inspectors opened our bundles and examined every candlestick, every feather bed, inside and out. They screamed questions at us. We couldn't understand what they said. They grabbed us by the arms and shoulders and pushed and shoved us where they wanted us to go.

I stood in a dark corner of a huge room. A woman in a uniform took scissors and cut off my two long braids, snip, snap, snip, snap. I shoved the braids into my coat pocket. She pulled my hair this way and that way, peering at my scalp.

Then she rolled up the sleeves of my dress. She stared at my arms. They were covered with spots. I hadn't taken my dress off the whole time I was on the ship. I hadn't even known I had a rash.

Did the rash mean I was sick? I couldn't understand what anyone was saying. They pushed and shoved me to a tall brick building with a thousand windows. Inside, the rooms were very white, so white they blinded my eyes, and very clean. They were the cleanest white rooms in the universe.

For days I lay on a white bed, wearing a white gown. I cried the whole time. I was sure they were going to send me back to the old country. What would I do there all alone?

After a week the rash had disappeared from my arms and they gave me back my clothes, all wrinkled, but clean.

A man came into the long white room. He looked familiar to me, but I didn't know who he was.

He walked over to my bed. "Fanny," he said, "don't you know me? Don't you know who I am?"

"Papa?" I whispered.

"Yes, Papa," he said. He put his arms around me and hugged me. I put my arms around him and hugged him back.

Then Papa took me home. He lived on Attorney Street, in a two-room apartment with his new wife. He worked in a garment factory where he earned three dollars a week.

The street was crowded with people and shops and peddlers and cats. Voices screamed from the windows. Laundry hung from the fire escapes.

Papa had said America was a golden land. I had thought that meant the streets were paved with gold. They weren't. They were paved with garbage—huge barrels so stuffed with old newspapers and rotting apples and potato peels that they overflowed—and wherever I walked, I stepped on something hard or rustly or squishy.

I went to school. I learned to speak English. I learned to read it and write it too. I went to the library. They gave you books for nothing. You had to bring them back, but when you did, they let you take others.

I made a friend. Her name was Selma and she went to P.S. 174, just like me. In the summer, if it was very hot, Selma and I slept outside on the fire escape.

Next door, Mrs. Ludwig sewed sleeves into coats. One day she said to me, "Fanny, if you take this bundle of coats to the factory for me, I'll give you two nickels."

"I'll take it for you, Mrs. Ludwig," I said. "I'll take it for you anywhere."

The bundle was so big I couldn't see over it. It was heavy too. But when I got back from the factory, Mrs. Ludwig gave me two nickels, just as she had promised. I looked at the nickels for a long time. Then I went back to our flat.

My father was sitting at the kitchen table. I held out my hand to him. The two nickels were lying in my palm. He looked up from the Yiddish paper he was reading. He saw the nickels in my hand. "Where did you get two nickels, Fanny?" he asked me.

"Mrs. Ludwig gave them to me because I took a bundle of coats over to the factory for her," I said. "They're for you."

Carefully he closed my fingers over the nickels. "No, tsatskeleh," he said, "they're for you."

I took one nickel and put it under my pillow. I would use it to go with Selma to see a Charlie Chaplin movie. The other nickel I held tight in my fist.

I ran out of our flat and down five flights of steps. I ran out on the street. A fruit peddler usually stood near the curb.

Yes, she was there. I rushed over to her. "Two oranges, please," I said. I held out my nickel.

She took the nickel. "Pick out your own oranges," she said. "Pick whichever oranges you want."

I stared at the oranges for a long time. Finally I chose the two that seemed to me to be the brightest, the largest, and the roundest.

Then I ran back into our building and up the five flights of steps to our flat. I put one orange on the table in front of my father. Then I sat down next to him. I peeled the other orange very, very slowly. I pulled it apart, section by section. I sucked each section until it was dry, and then I chewed and swallowed what was left. It tasted like heaven.

If at that very moment a gate had opened, and on the other side of the gate were the wild gooseberries and little brown pears of Rohatyn, I would not have walked through that gate.

I was already home.